Hot
Chocolate

Victoria Blakemore

To Mrs. G, for always being there to listen to my new book ideas!

vblakemore.author@gmail.com

Copyright info/picture credits

Cover, Ruslan Mitin/AdobeStock; Page 3, Storyblocks; Page 5, Storyblocks; Page 7, gate74/Pixabay; Page 9, skeeze/Pixabay; Page 11, bigacis/AdobeStock; Page 13, thecakeschool/Pixabay; Page 15, Storyblocks; Page 17, Storyblocks; Page 19, Andrey Kiselev/AdobeStock; Page 21, Storyblocks; Page 23; Storyblocks; Page 25, Storyblocks; Page 27, vinzling/Pixabay; Page 29, Storyblocks; Page 31, TerriC/Pixabay; Page 33, Ruslan Mitin/AdobeStock

Table of Contents

What is Hot Chocolate?

Hot chocolate is a rich, sweet drink that many people enjoy. It has been used in many ways over the years.

While hot chocolate is originally from Central America, it is now enjoyed all over the world.

Today, hot chocolate is made in

the winter as a sweet way to

warm up when it is cold outside.

Ingredients

Hot chocolate is made from pieces or shavings of chocolate. It can be made with water, but it is richer and creamier when made with milk.

The chocolate is melted into hot water or milk. Hot cocoa is made by mixing cocoa powder into hot water or milk.

Cacao Beans

Cacao beans come from the Theobroma, or cacao, tree. They are found inside large pods that grow on the tree.

Before they can be made into chocolate, the beans must be dried and roasted. Then, they can be ground into a chocolate **paste**.

Cacao beans are used to make things like chocolate, cocoa powder, and cocoa butter.

Dark Chocolate

Dark chocolate is made with cocoa butter. It is not as sweet as milk chocolate, which is made with milk butter. It has more of a **bitter** taste.

When made with dark chocolate, hot chocolate is not as sweet as when it is made with milk chocolate.

Hot chocolate that is made

with dark chocolate is healthier

than when it is made with other

kinds of chocolate.

History

Hot chocolate was first made by the Olmec, Aztec, and Mayan people of Central America.

They would roast cacao seeds, then remove the nib and grind it into a paste. The chocolate paste would be mixed with hot water.

Cacao nibs are part of cacao seeds. They have been dried, cleaned, roasted, and removed from their shell.

Spanish explorers brought cacao seeds back to Spain with them. The seeds were traded and sold to other countries in Europe.

Cacao seeds were **rare** and expensive. This meant that hot chocolate was enjoyed by royals and people with a lot of money.

This changed when a Dutch

inventor found a way to make

cocoa powder from cacao

beans.

Special Ceremonies

Originally, the people of Central America used hot chocolate for special **ceremonies**.

The hot chocolate was used more as a medicine or a way to improve wisdom and find guidance.

In Central America, chili

peppers were often added to

hot chocolate.

Hot Chocolate Houses

When hot chocolate was brought to Europe, it was very popular among people with lots of money.

It was used at special events and in "chocolate houses." They were like coffee shops, but with hot chocolate instead.

Hot chocolate is much easier

to get now. Many people

make it in their homes.

Expeditions

In 1911, hot chocolate was brought on an **expedition** to the South Pole. It was led by Roald Amundsen.

The hot chocolate provided the explorers with lots of **calories**. It also helped to keep them warm in the **frigid** temperatures of the South Pole.

During war time, cocoa nibs were

given to soldiers because it was

thought to give them strength.

Hot Cocoa

The hot chocolate that most people make with cocoa powder is actually called hot cocoa. It is usually thinner and sweeter than hot chocolate.

The cocoa powder used to make hot cocoa is very sweet. It is usually higher in sugar than hot chocolate.

Hot cocoa mixes are sold in stores. Some of them are plain hot cocoa, others have marshmallows in the packet.

Toppings

While some people drink their hot chocolate or hot cocoa plain, others like to add toppings to their drink.

Some toppings are used to add new flavors. Others are used to make hot chocolate or hot cocoa sweeter.

Marshmallows are a common
opping. They make hot chocolate
or hot cocoa even sweeter.

Whipped cream can also add more sweetness, as can chocolate syrup or caramel.

Cinnamon is another common topping. It adds a new spicy flavor to a sweet drink. It is sometimes **combined** with a caramel sauce.

Many people like to add more

than just one topping, trying

different flavor **combinations**.

Nutrition

The nutrition of hot chocolate depends on how it is made. When made with dark chocolate, it is not as high in sugar or fat as when it is made with milk chocolate.

When made with milk, it is high in nutrients such as calcium and iron.

Any toppings like marshmallows or

whipped cream can add more

sugar and fat.

Health Benefits

When made with milk and dark chocolate, hot chocolate can help to lower blood pressure. This can help to keep your heart healthy.

It can also help to **soothe** your throat if you have a cough.

Hot chocolate made with dark

chocolate is the healthiest kind. It

is better for you than hot cocoa.

Recipes

Hot Cocoa

Ingredients:

1/4 cup cocoa powder   4 cups milk

1/2 cup sugar   1/3 cup hot water

3/4 tsp. vanilla extract   dash salt

Directions:

1. Stir cocoa, sugar, and salt in saucepan. Add water and bring to a boil.

2. Lower heat and add milk. Add vanilla and stir until mixed.

3. Serve topped with marshmallows, cinnamon, or whipped cream.

Hot Chocolate

Ingredients:

8 cups milk   1 tsp. vanilla extract

1/4 cup sugar

16 oz. semisweet chocolate chips

Directions:

1. Combine all ingredients in medium saucepan.

2. Heat on medium until liquid begins to simmer.

3. Mix with whisk until chocolate is melted and mixture is smooth.

4. Serve topped with marshmallows, cinnamon, or whipped cream.

Glossary

Bitter: having a sharp taste, not sweet

Calories: units of energy

Ceremony: a series of acts to honor a special event

Combination: things that were brought together or combined

Combined: put together

Expedition: a journey taken for

a special reason

Frigid: very cold, freezing

Paste: a thick, wet mixture

Rare: hard to get or find

About the Author

Victoria Blakemore is a first grade

teacher in Southwest Florida with a

passion for reading.

You can visit her at

www.elementaryexplorers.com

Also in This Series

ray Wolves	Sloths	Flamingos	Camels	Koalas	Honey Bees	Pandas
Pangolins	White-Tailed Deer	Orcas	Giraffes	Corn	Meerkats	Echidnas
Walruses	Raccoons	Bald Eagles	Apples	Arctic Foxes	Red Pandas	Cassowaries
Tigers	Ladybugs	Moose	Beluga Whales	Leopards	Elephants	Jellyfish
Binturongs	Lions	Dolphins	Reindeer	Hammerhead Sharks	Hippos	Pumpkins
Peafowl	Chameleons	Florida Panthers	Aye-Ayes	Black Bears	Cheetahs	Manatees
Gingerbread	Polar Bears	Hot Chocolate	Orangutans	Coyotes	Marshmallows	Strawberries

Also in This Series

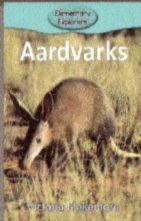

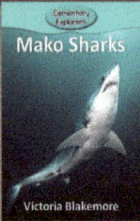

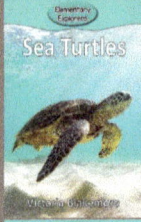

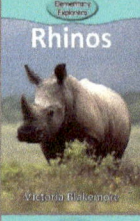

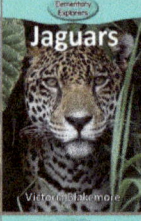

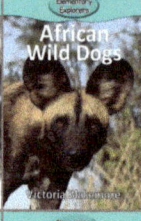

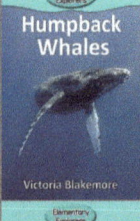

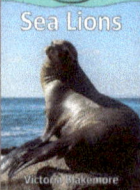

Aardvarks	Mako Sharks	Alligators	Frogs	Hedgehogs	Brown Bears	Bongos
Sea Turtles	Quokkas	Muskrats	Zebras	Red Foxes	Ring-Tailed Lemurs	Platypuses
Anteaters	Kangaroos	Rhinos	Jaguars	Wombats	Capybaras	Gorillas
Cats	Skunks	Butterflies	Dingoes	Snow Leopards	African Wild Dogs	Penguins
Whale Sharks	Wolverines	Warthogs	Caracals	Badgers	Seals	Hummingbirds
Pikas	Humpback Whales	Pumas	Lemonade	Llamas	Tulips	Ostriches
Sunflowers	Fennec Foxes	Sea Lions	Squirrels	Roses	Porcupines	Ice Cream

Elementary Explorers — Victoria Blakemore